THEORY MADE EASY
FOR LITTLE CHILDREN

LEVEL 2

Lina Ng

Let's move on together for a more "MUSICAL" music education for the new generation.
The **ART of Teaching (AoT)** is very much suited to be used alongside all piano tutor books and graded syllabus.
Everything in music is interconnected.
You may play the **Musical Moments** series for **more making connections ideas and activities**.
Remember to include **AURAL TRAINING** when teaching **theory** - "**HEAR**" the **theory** (refer to **AoT** for suggested **ideas**).

© RHYTHM MP SDN. BHD. 1995
New Edition: 2010

Published by
RHYTHM MP SDN. BHD.
1947, Lorong IKS Bukit Minyak 2,
Taman IKS Bukit Minyak, 14100 Simpang Ampat,
Penang, Malaysia.
Tel: +60 4 5050246 (Direct Line), +60 4 5073690 (Hunting Line)
E-mail: RhythmMP@mphsb.com
Website: www.RhythmMP.com
Follow us on Facebook.com/MusicJamboree

Cover Design & Illustrations by
LIM WAI FUN

ISBN 967-985-445-0
Order No.: MPT-3005-02

Photocopying Prohibited.
All rights reserved. Unauthorised reproduction
of any part of this publication by any means
including photocopying is an infringement of copyright.

Contents

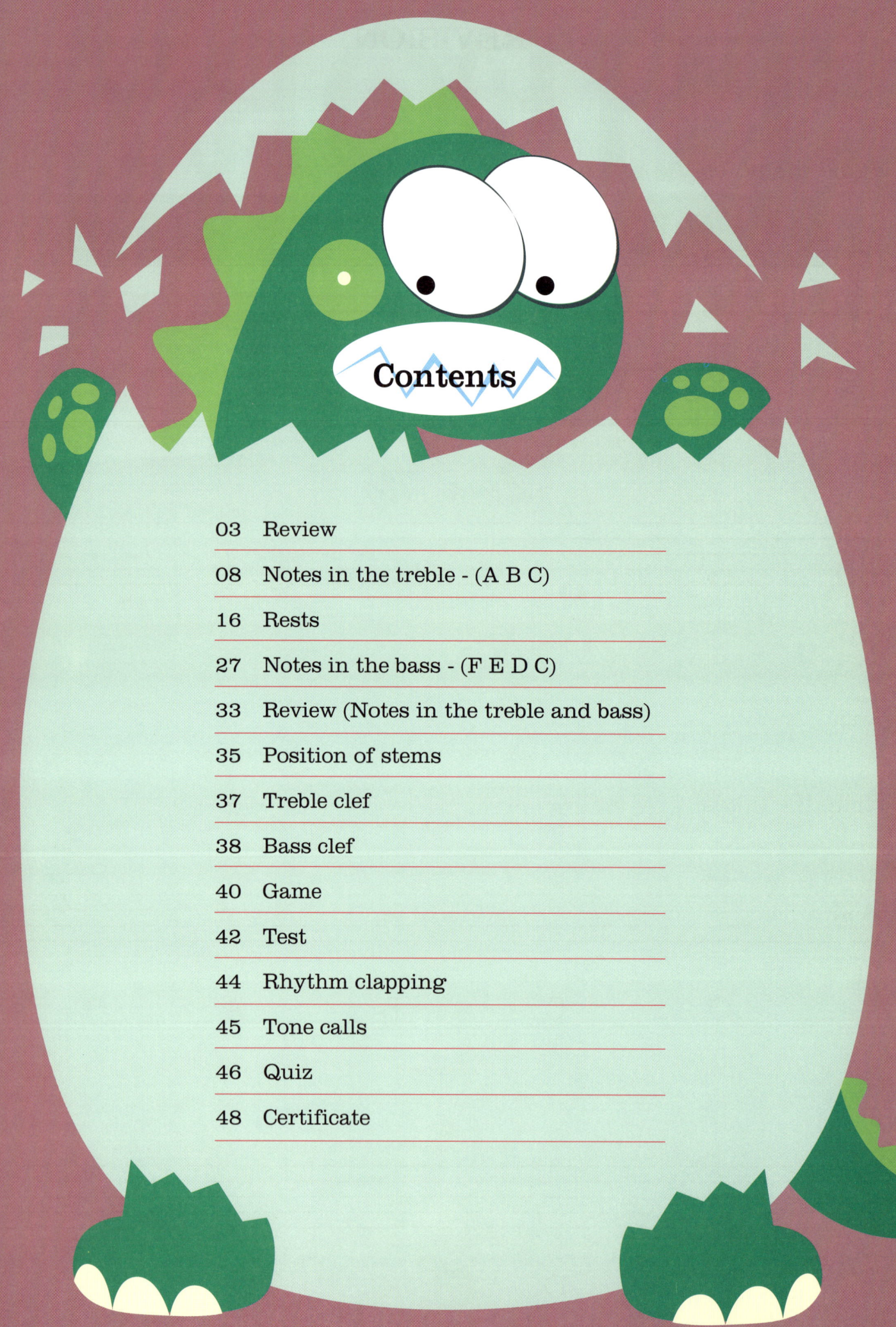

03	Review
08	Notes in the treble - (A B C)
16	Rests
27	Notes in the bass - (F E D C)
33	Review (Notes in the treble and bass)
35	Position of stems
37	Treble clef
38	Bass clef
40	Game
42	Test
44	Rhythm clapping
45	Tone calls
46	Quiz
48	Certificate

REVISION

Name the notes.

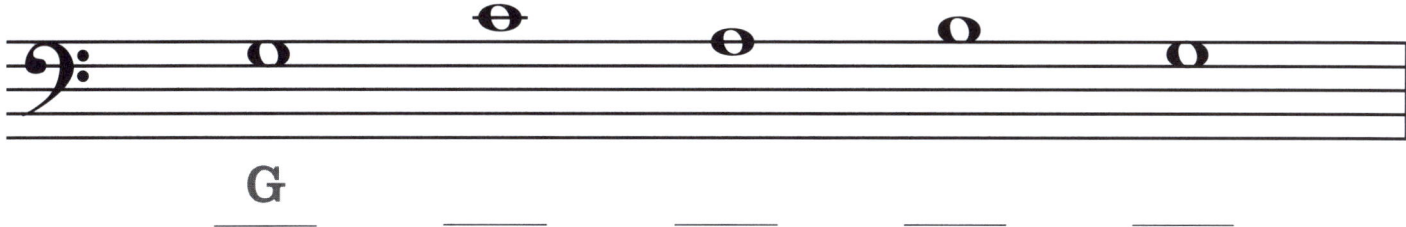

G _____ _____ _____ _____

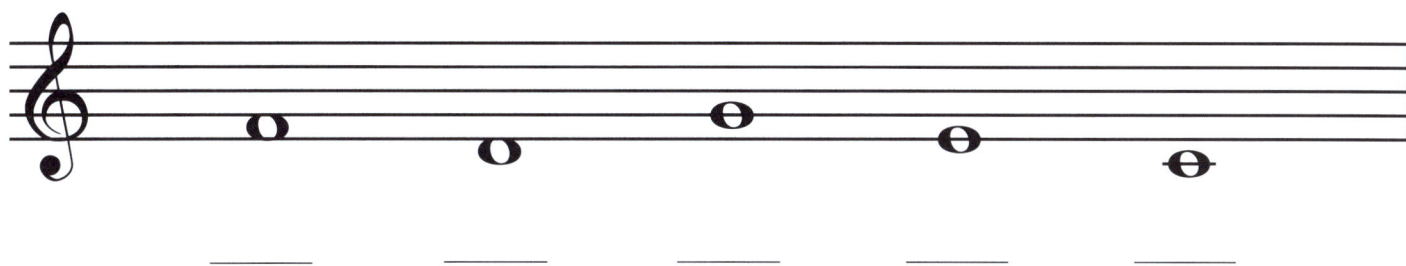

_____ _____ _____ _____ _____

Write the notes.

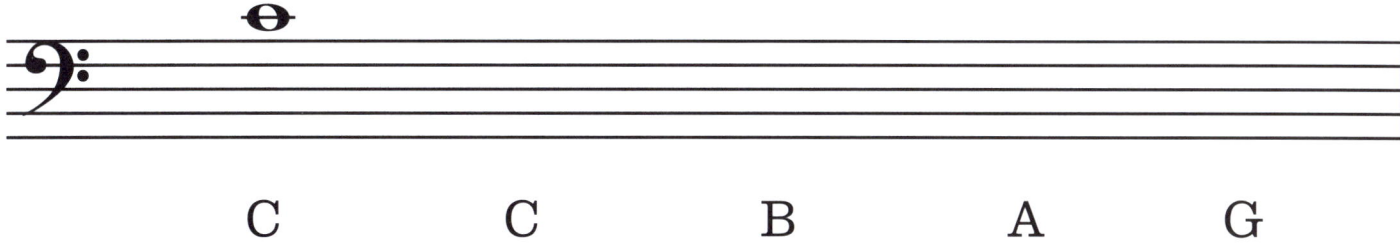

C C B A G

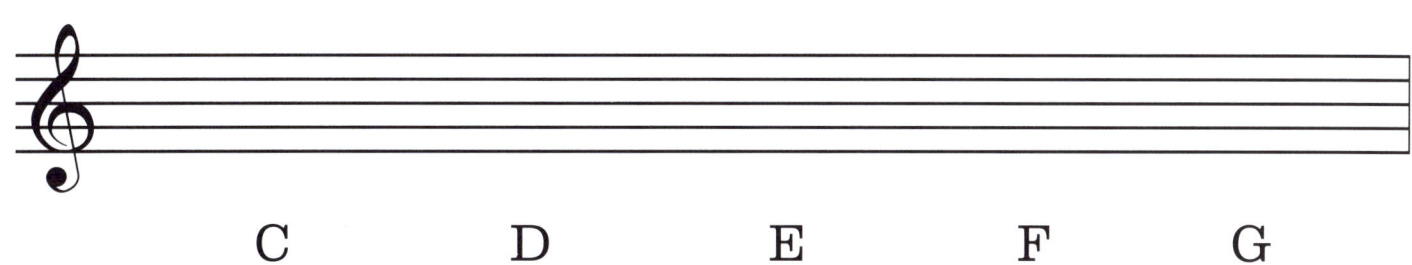

C D E F G

Match the following.

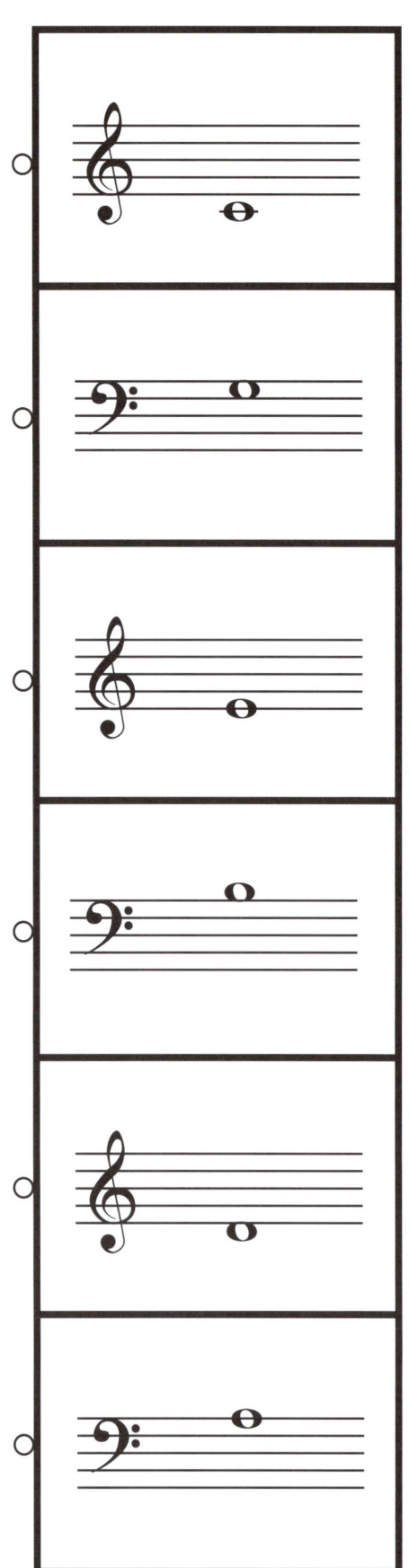

Paste stickers of the correct time signature.

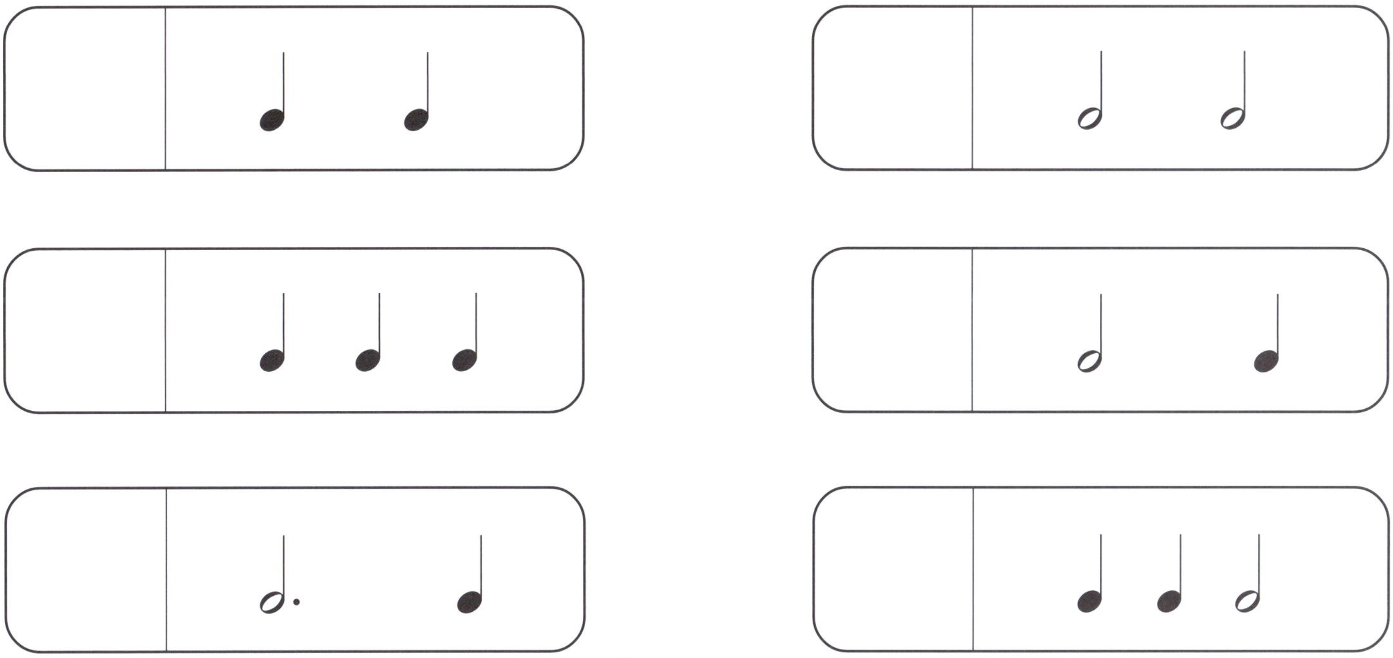

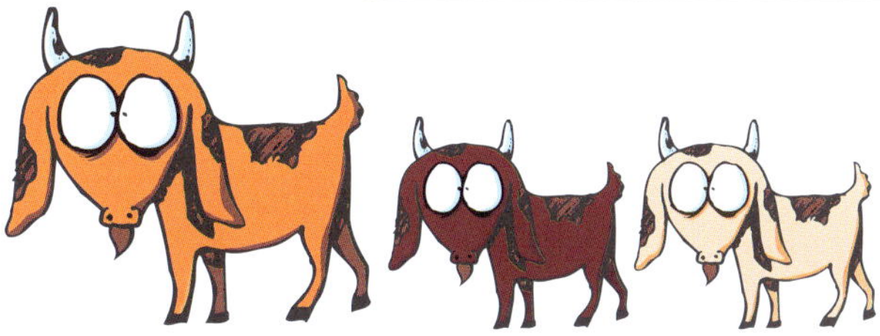

Write the counts.

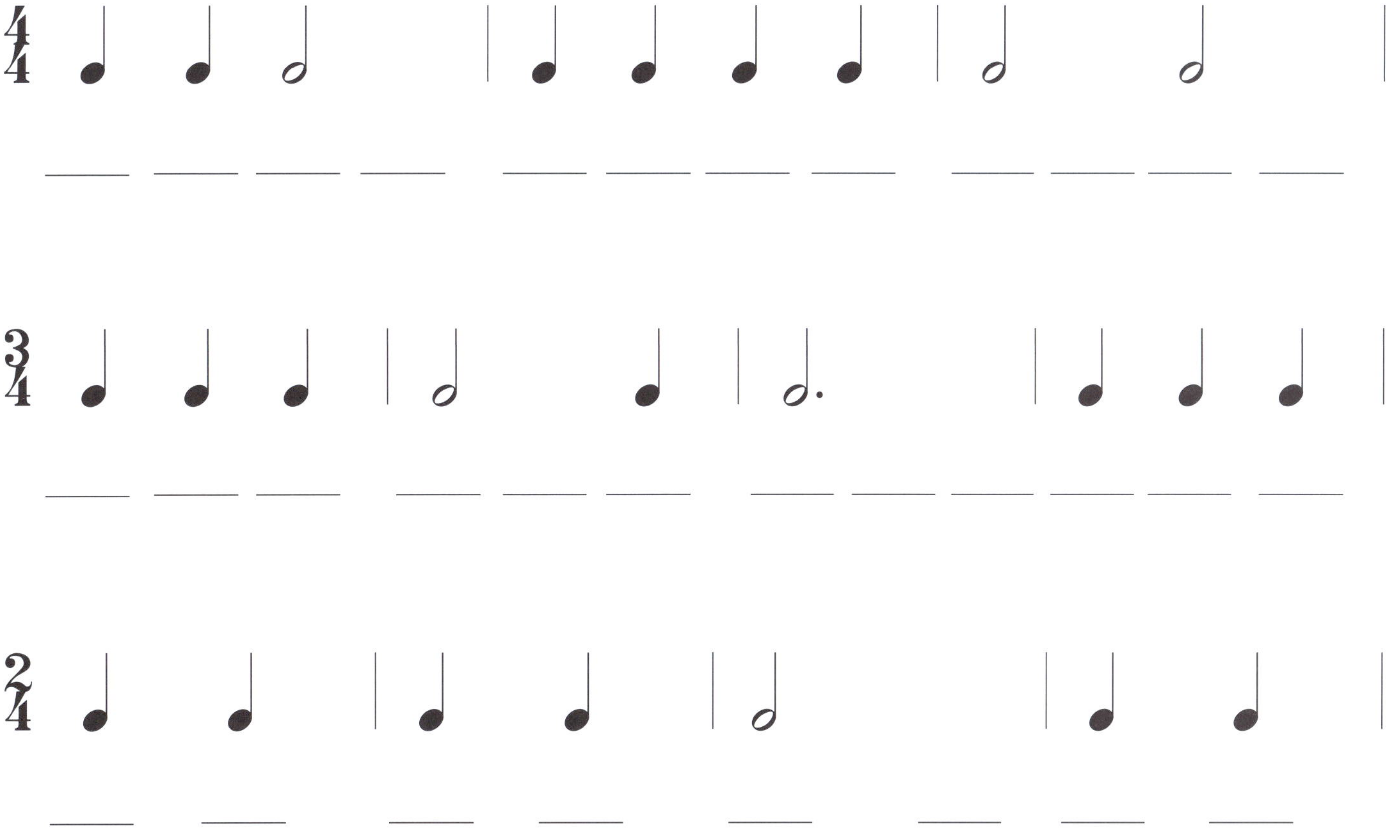

Complete each bar with a note.

Use stickers.

RED RIDING HOOD

Follow the notes ♩ ♩ ♩. o and see where Little Red Riding Hood is going.

NOTES IN THE TREBLE
A B C

Ant

A for Ant.

A A A A A A A

A

Match the notes to the correct alphabets.

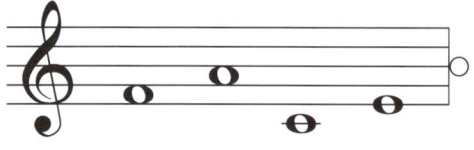

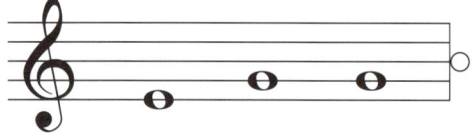

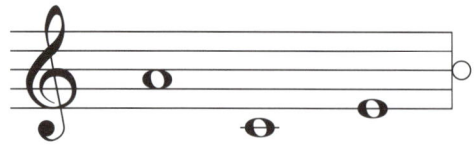

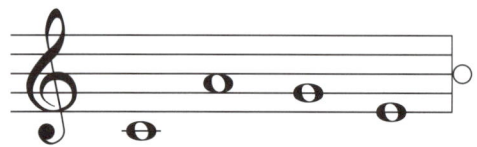

EGG

ACE

CAGE

FACE

B for Bird.

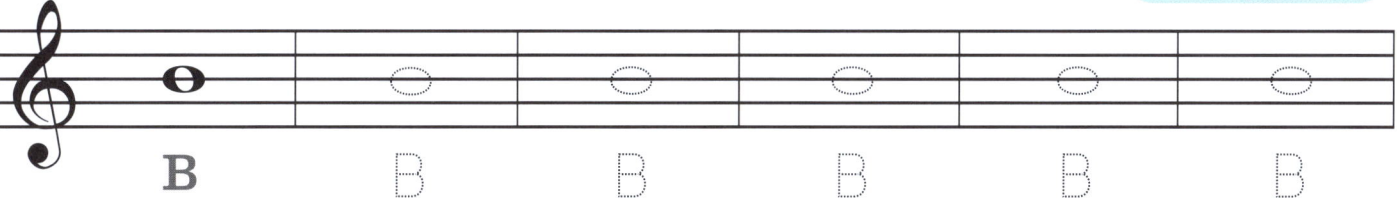

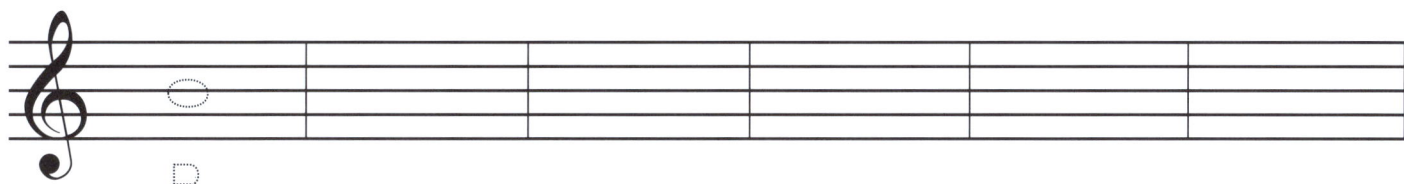

C for Cow.

Name the notes.

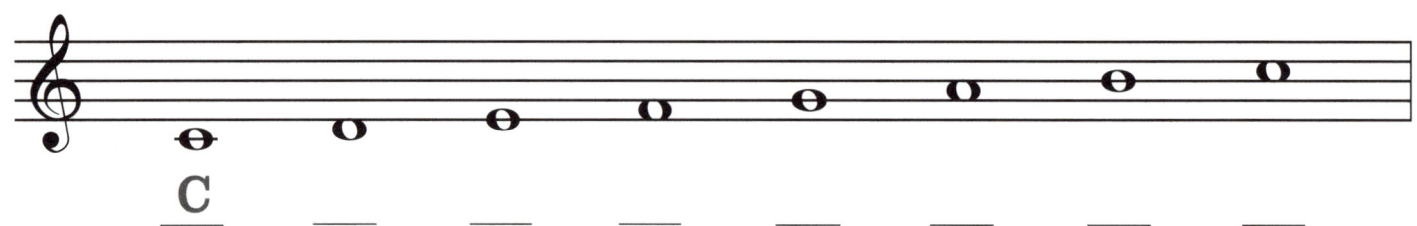

Write the notes.

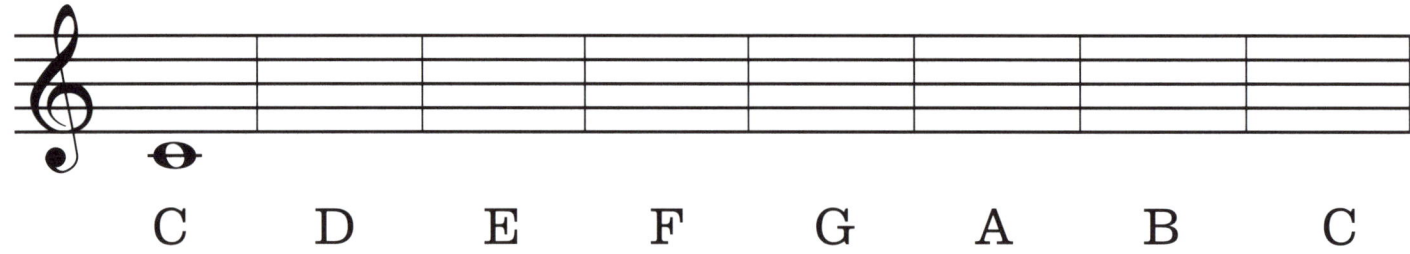

C D E F G A B C

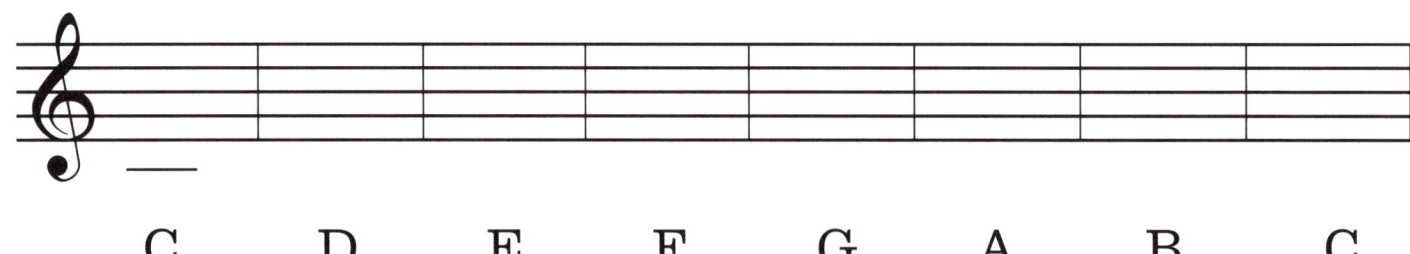

C D E F G A B C

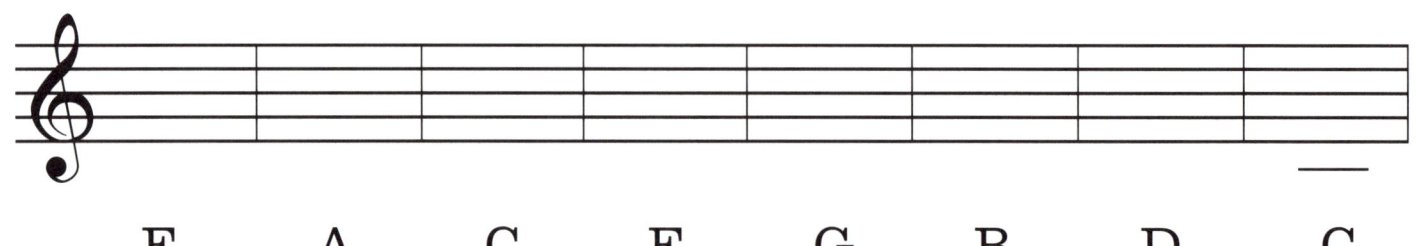

F A C E G B D C

Prefix the sticker where required.

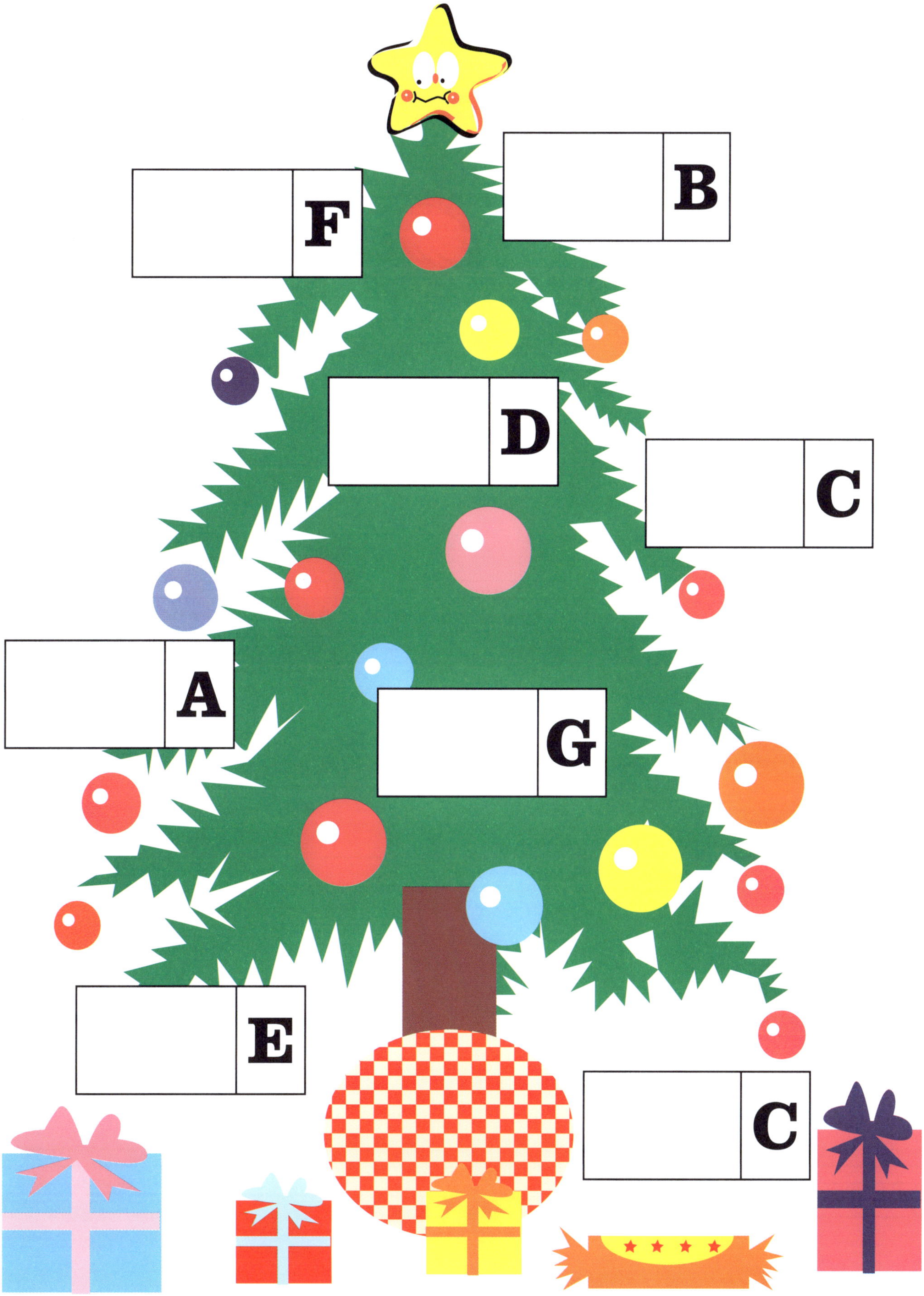

Write the notes.

Colour on the keyboard the notes you have to play.

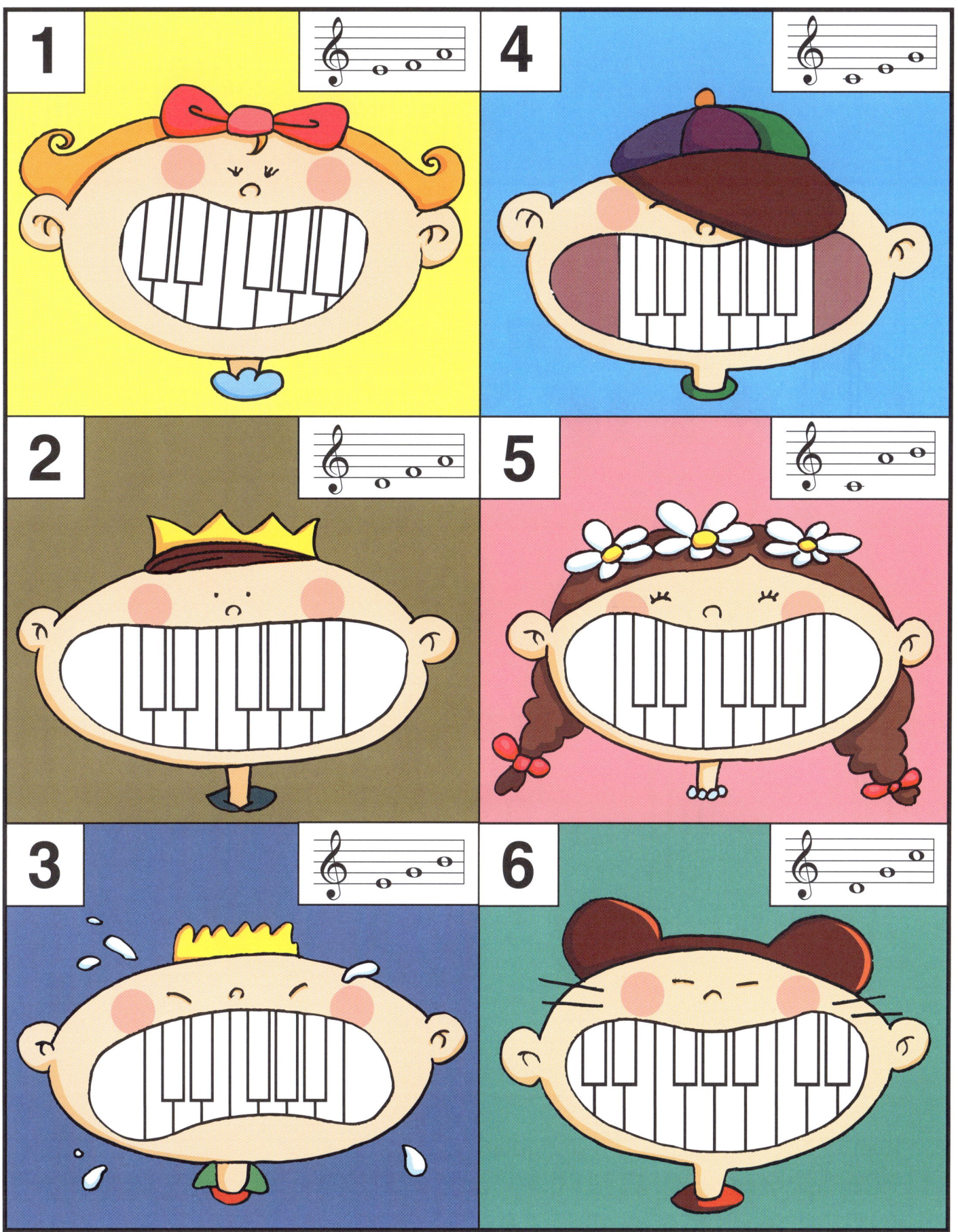

Help the girls find their partners.
Colour their skirts as follows.

B note - Blue   A note - Red   C note - Yellow

Paste the notes named.

Treble notes　　　　　　　　　　　　　　　　　Bass notes

C

B

A

G

RESTS

NAME	NOTE	COUNTS	REST
Semibreve	𝅝	4	𝄻
Minim	𝅗𝅥	2	𝄼
Crotchet	♩	1	𝄽

Copy the rests.

4

2

1

Level 2

Write the counts.

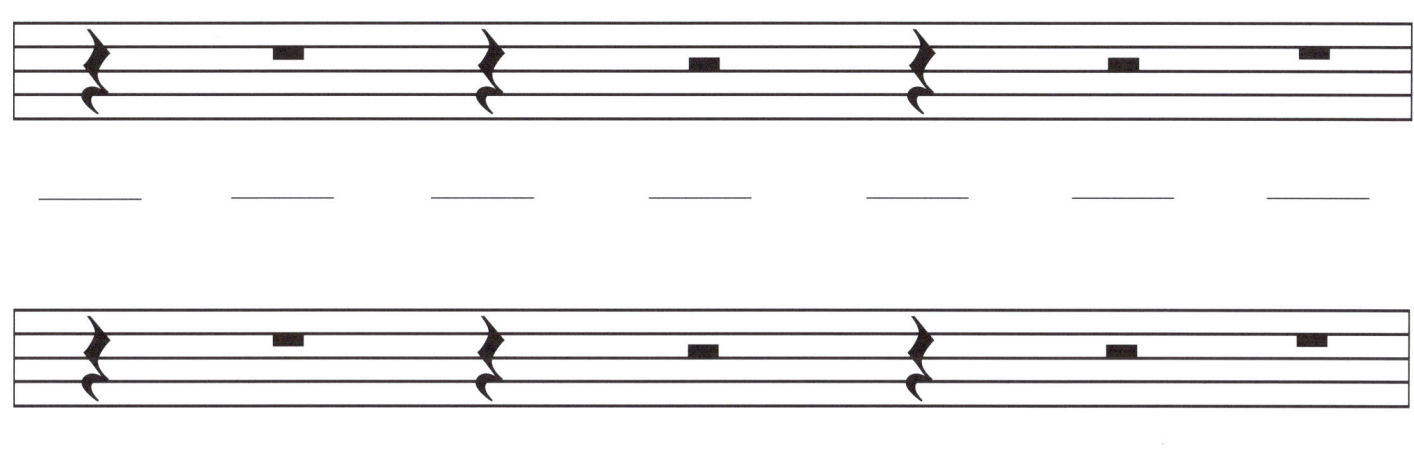

Prefix a rest of the same value.

1		4	
2		1	
4		2	
1		4	

Colour the circles to show the number of counts.
(1 circle = 1 count)

Put a tick (✓) where true and a cross (✗) where false.

♩	+	𝄽	=	2		✓
𝅗𝅥	+	𝄽	=	4		
𝄻	+	♩	=	3		
♩	+	𝄻	=	4		
𝅝	+	𝄽	=	5		
𝄻	+	♩.	=	5		
♩.	+	𝄻	=	4		
𝄼	+	𝅗𝅥	=	7		

Level 2

Help Mr. Brown find his family.
Colour according to the number of counts.

Red = 4   Yellow = 2   Green = 3   Brown = 1

Paste stickers of the correct value.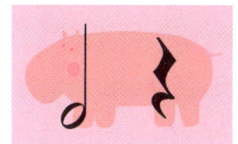

4/4		3/4	
4/4		3/4	
4/4		3/4	
4/4		2/4	
4/4		2/4	

22

Paste bar-lines to the following. |

Paste stickers of the correct time signature. 2/4

Write the counts.

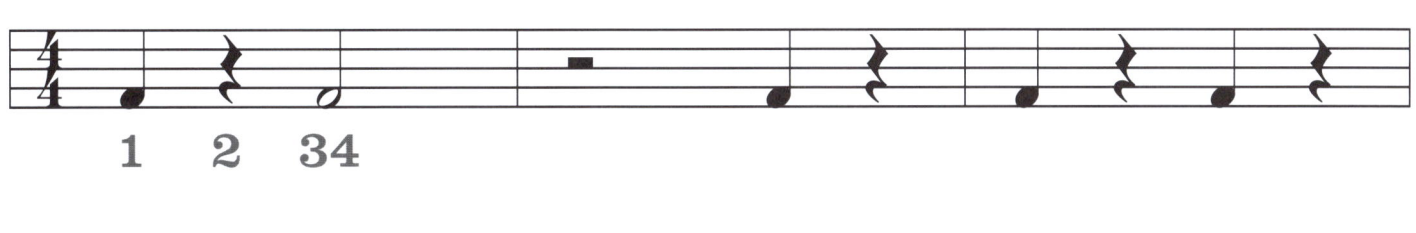

Insert bar-lines.

Complete each bar with a rest. Use stickers. For an empty bar, use the bar-rest whether it is 2/4, 3/4 or 4/4 time.

Level 2

1. Look at the time signature.
2. Pick out one note or rest that does not belong to the group.
3. Cover it up with a sticker.

 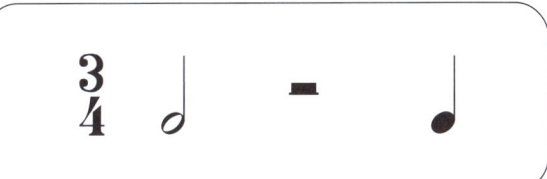

 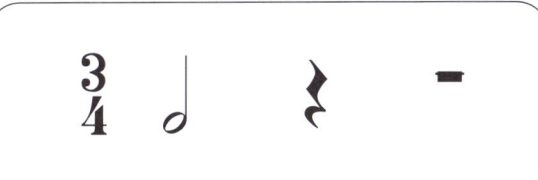

 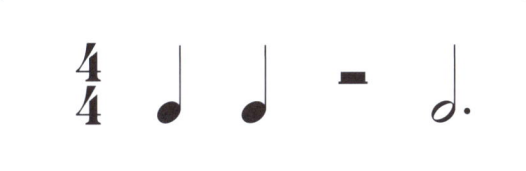

Level 2

1. Look at the time signature.
2. Circle one more note or rest to complete the time.
3. The first one has been done for you.

NOTES IN THE BASS
F E D C

F for Frog.

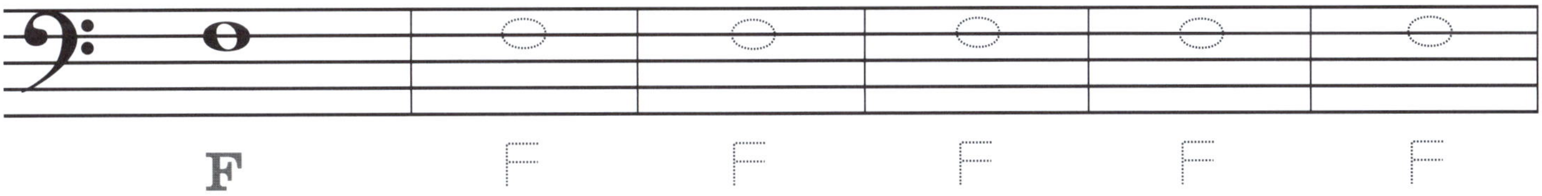

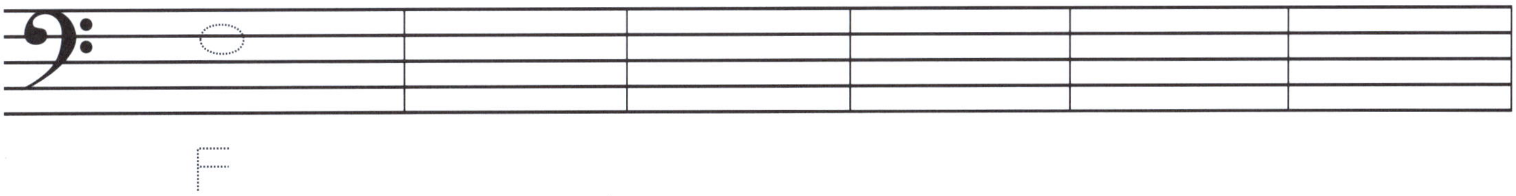

E for Egg.

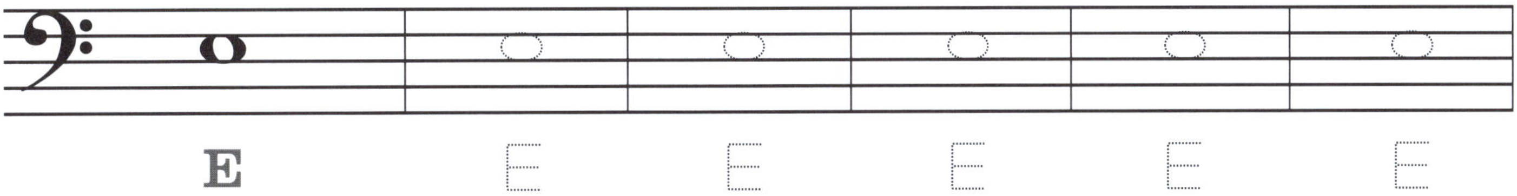

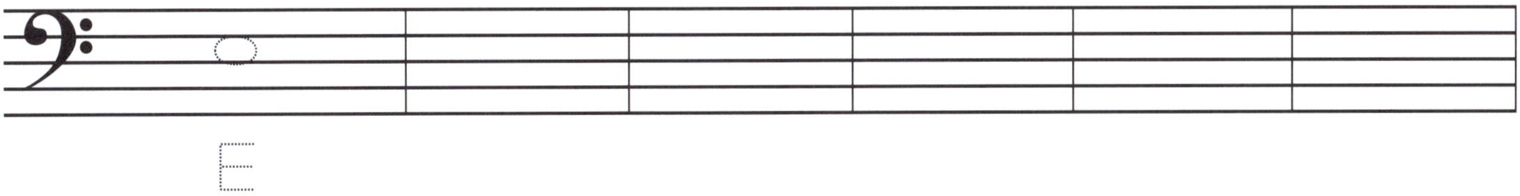

Level 2

Write the notes.

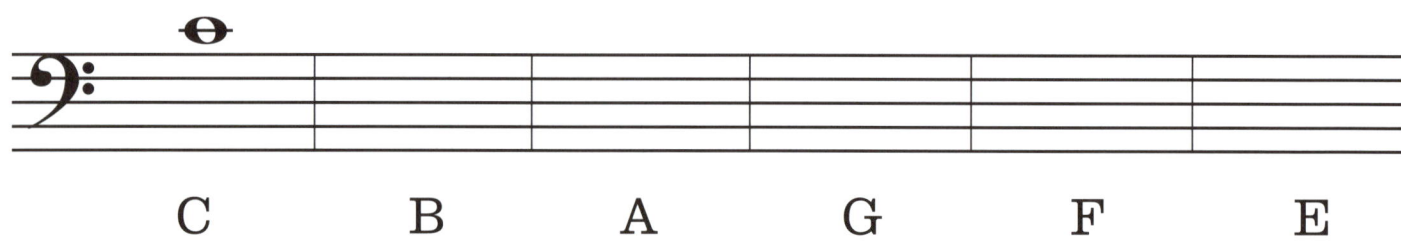

Name the notes.

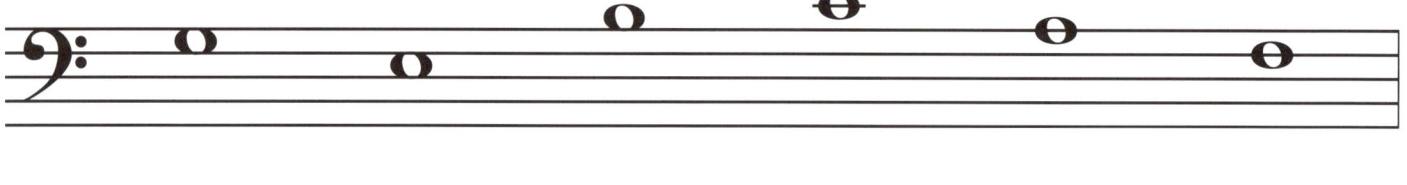

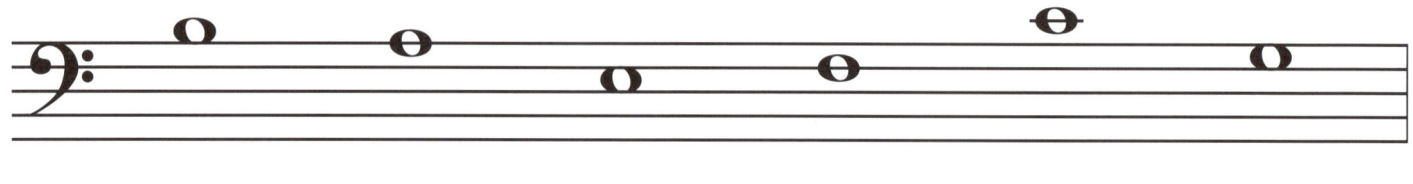

D for Duck.

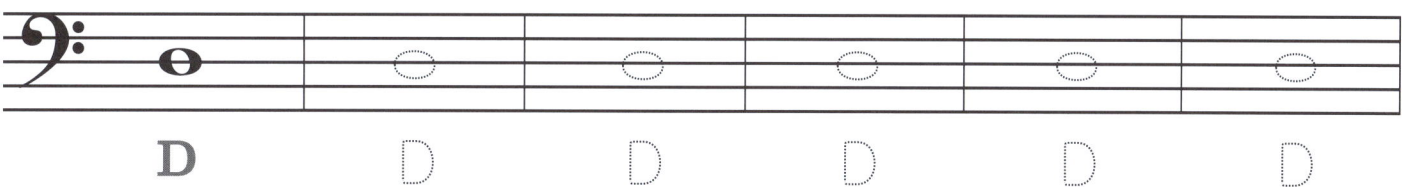

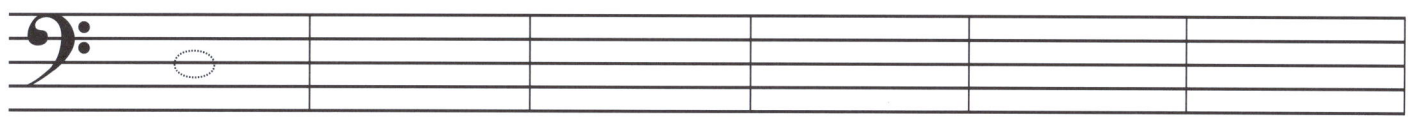

C for Car.

TREASURE HUNT

The girls are on a treasure hunt.
Follow their routes and answer the questions.

Who will find the treasure?		Miss ____

Who will meet each other?		Miss ____ & Miss ____

Who will be lost in the woods?		Miss ____

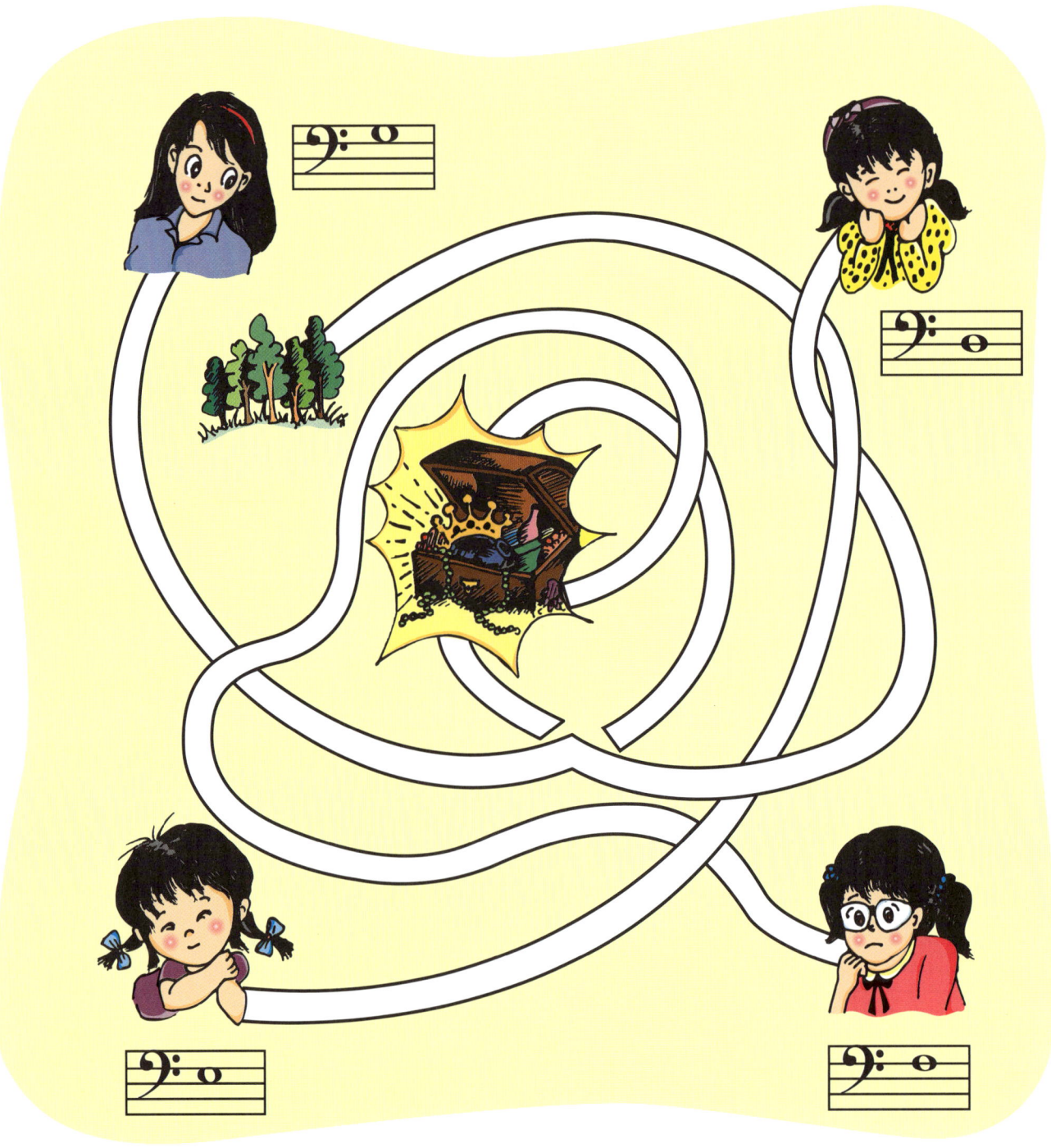

Level 2

Match the notes to the alphabets.

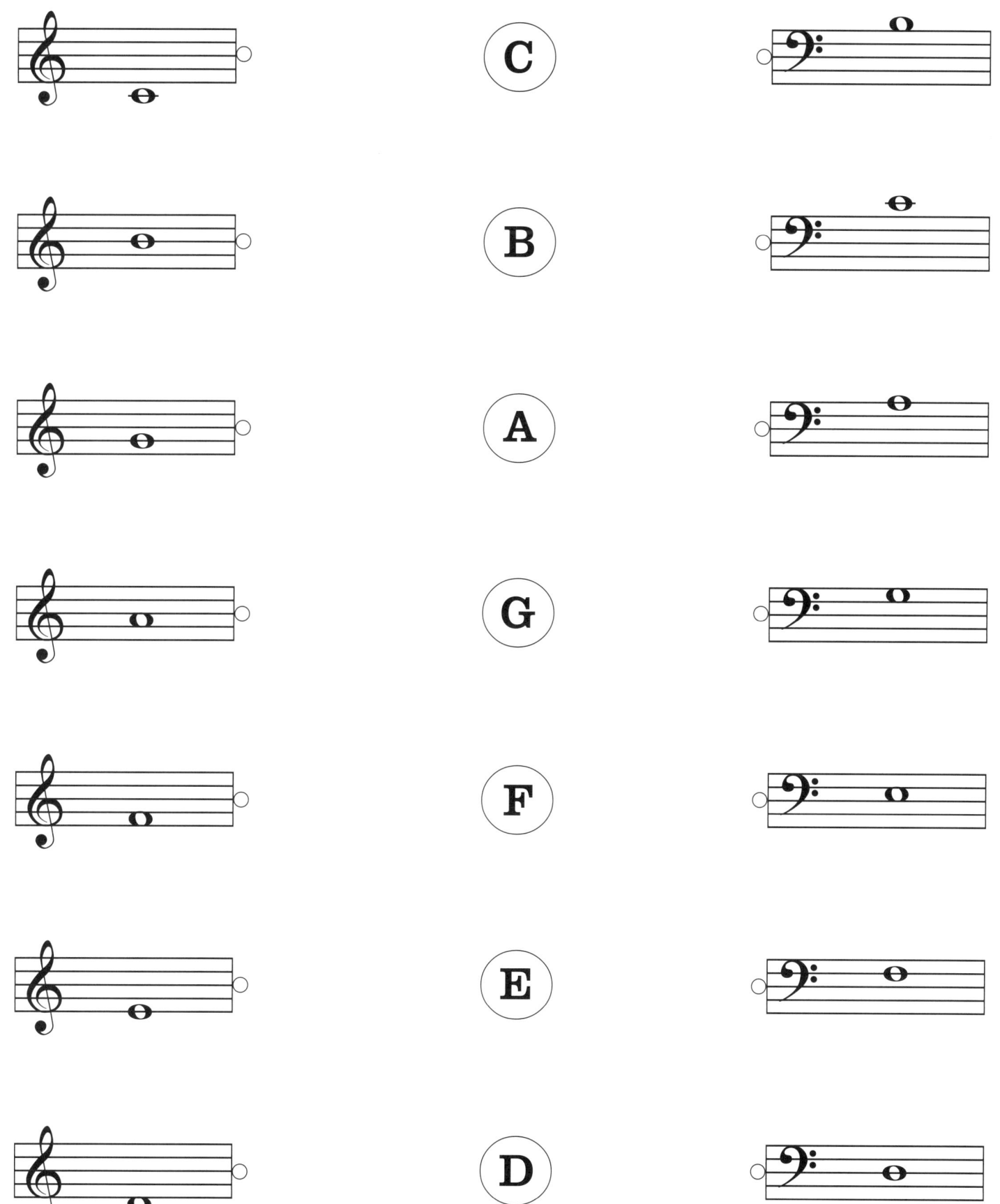

Colour on the keyboard the notes you have to play.

REVISION
NOTES IN THE TREBLE AND BASS

Cover the wrong name with a sticker.

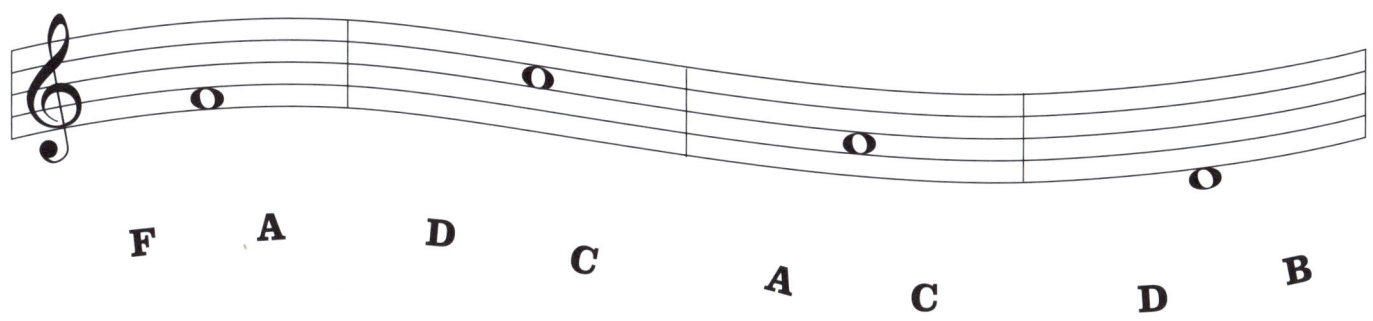

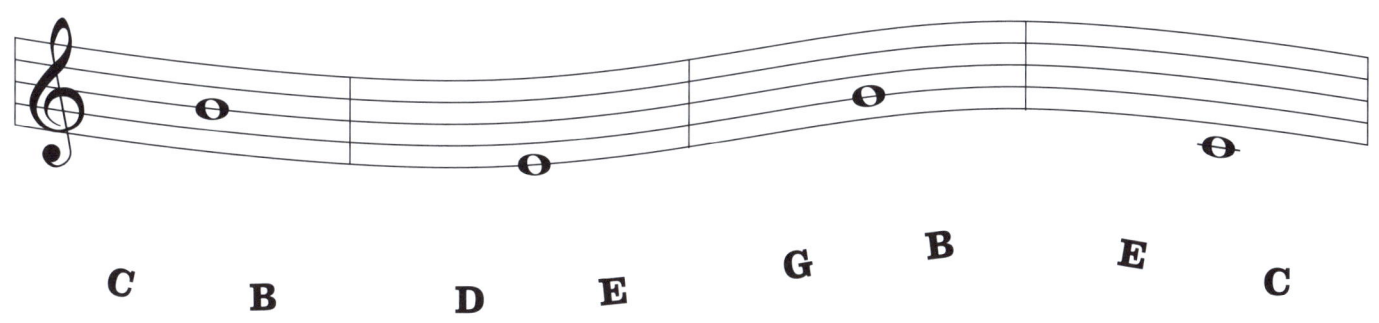

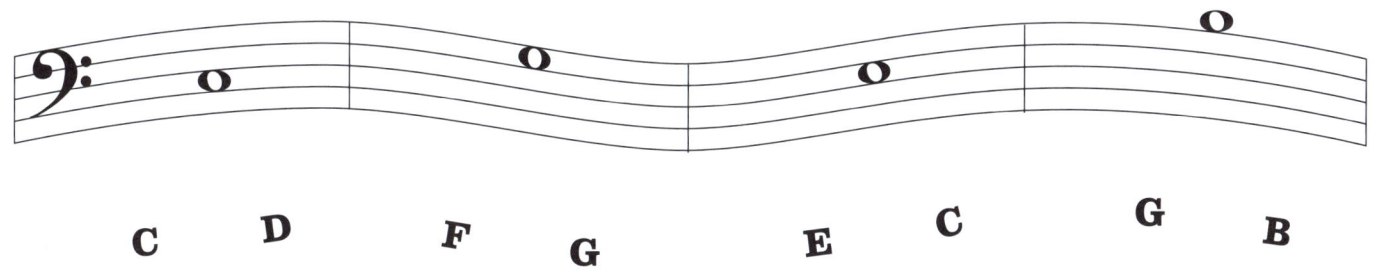

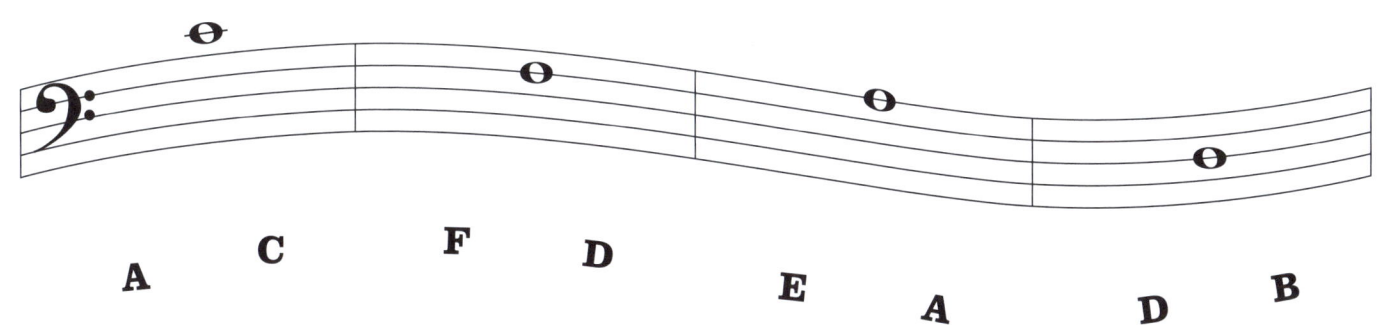

34

1. Name the notes.

2. Paste the sticker with the same name.

TREBLE NOTES	NAME	BASS NOTES
𝄞 o	G	
𝄞 o		
𝄞 o		
𝄞 o		
𝄞 o		
𝄞 o		
𝄞 o		
𝄞 o		

Level 2

POSITION OF STEMS

The stems indicate either ⬚ p ⬚ or ⬚ d ⬚ Pond

stems up   up or down   stems down

Add a stem to every note.

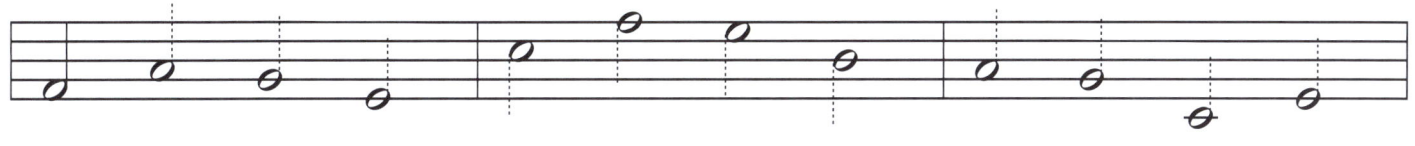

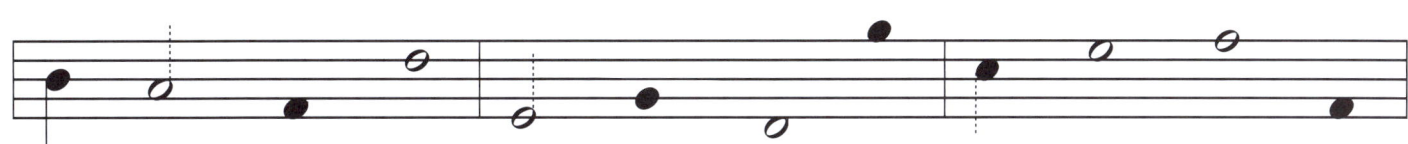

Level 2

TREBLE CLEF

This is also called the 'G clef'.
It cuts the G line.

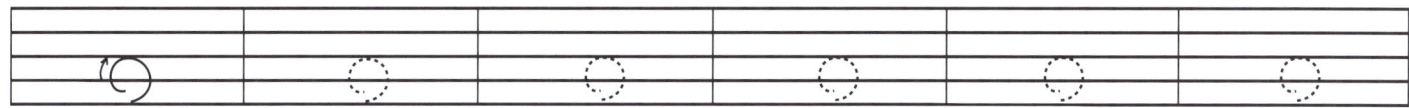

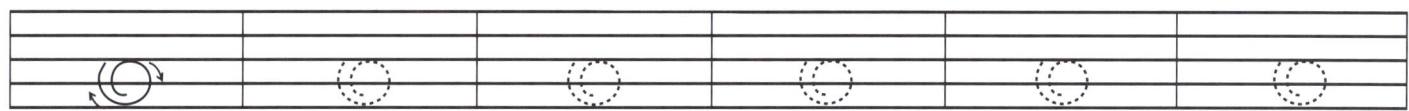

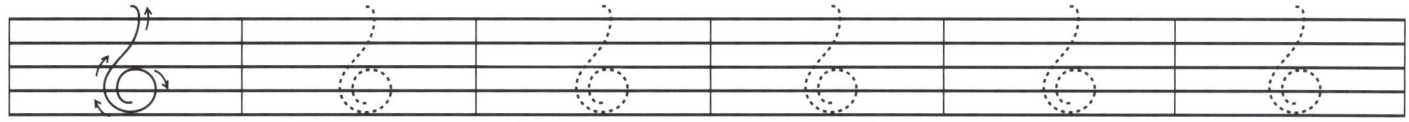

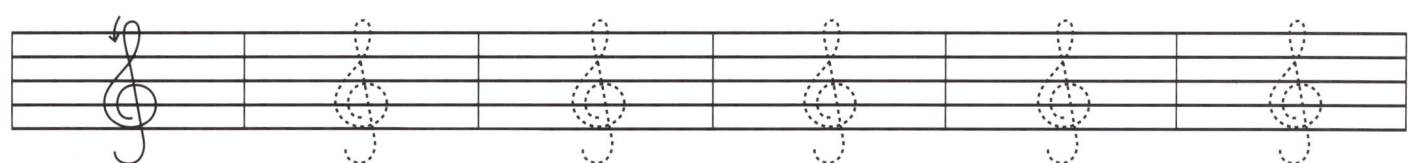

Level 2

BASS CLEF

This is also called the 'F clef'.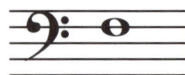

In each group, only one is correct.
Colour the correct ones.

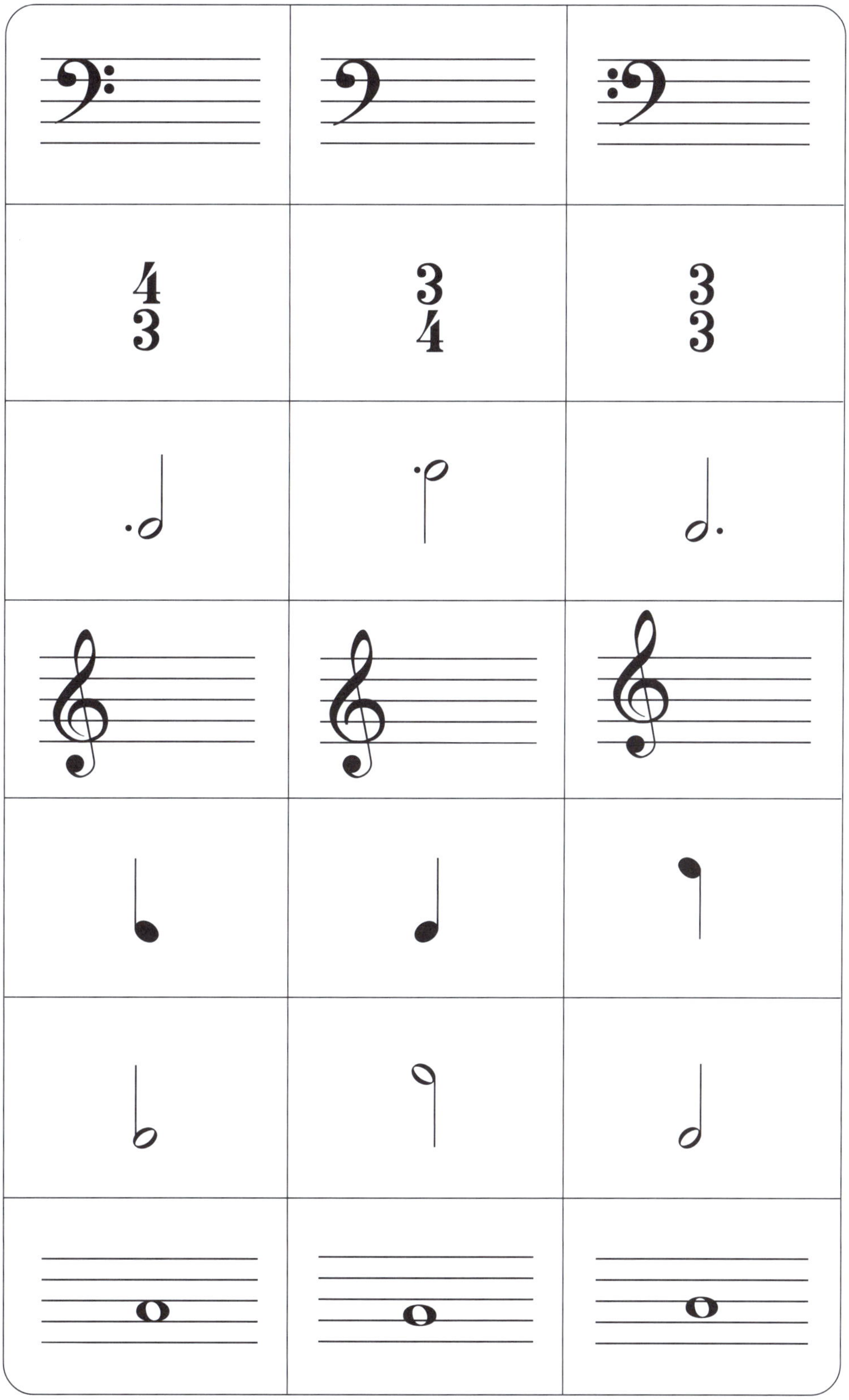

GAME

1. Look at Picture A.
2. Look at Picture B.

Picture A

In picture B there are many extras. Circle the extras in red.

Picture B

TEST

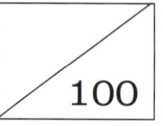

Date: _____

1. Write the number of counts. (1, 2, 3, 4)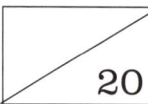

____   ____   ____   ____   ____

____   ____   ____   ____   ____

2. Name the notes.

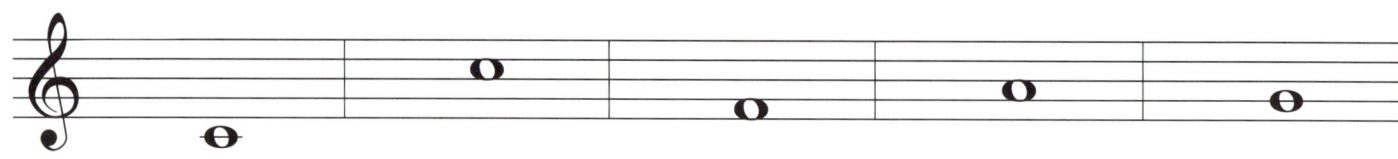

____   ____   ____   ____   ____

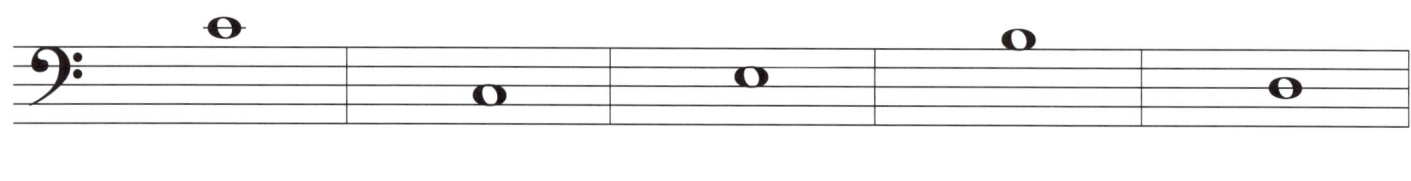

____   ____   ____   ____   ____

3. Label the 10 white keys on the keyboard.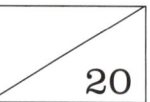

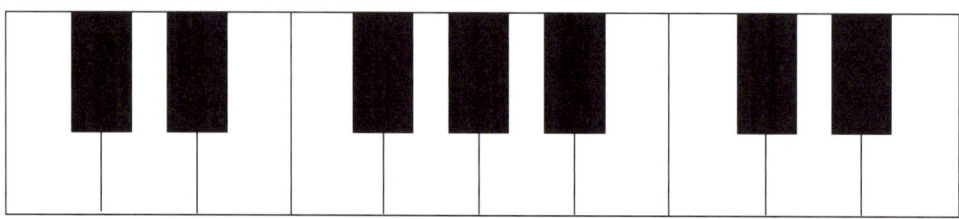

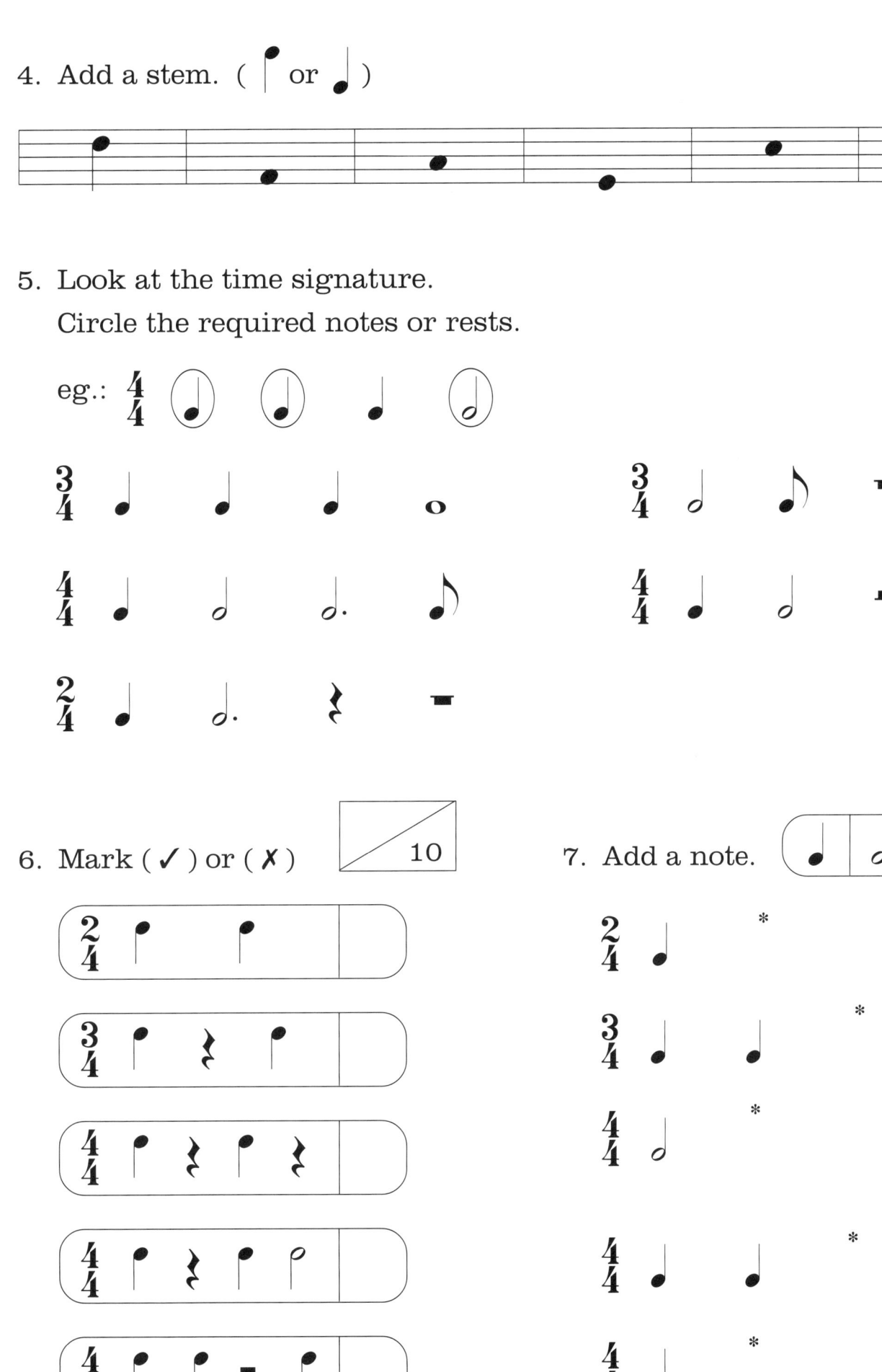

RHYTHM CLAPPING

Teacher claps a rhythm pattern and count aloud 1 2 3 4. Pupil imitates.

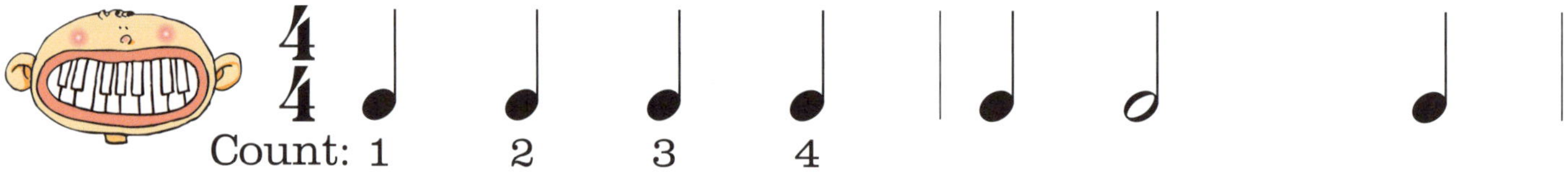

Count: 1 2 3 4

Write your own rhythm. Clap it and count aloud 1 2 3 4.

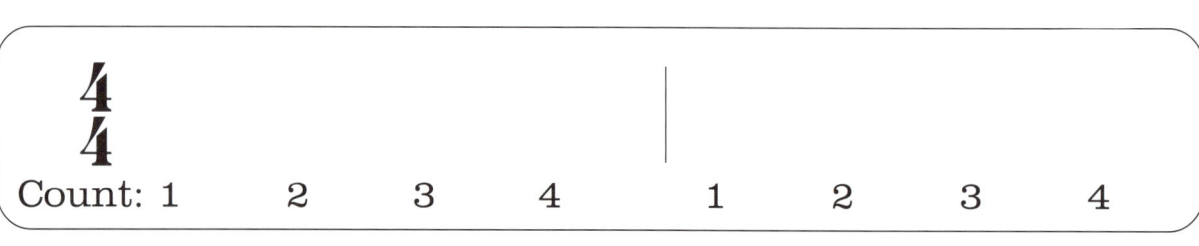

Count: 1 2 3 4 1 2 3 4

Level 2

TONE CALLS

45

Teacher sings any example below. Pupil imitates.

1.
2.
3.
4.
5.
6.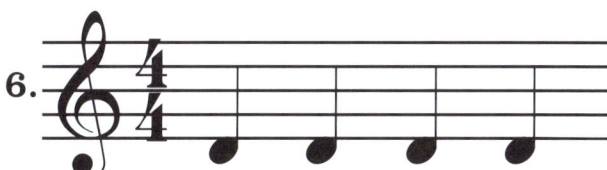
7.
8.

Write your own melody. Then sing it.

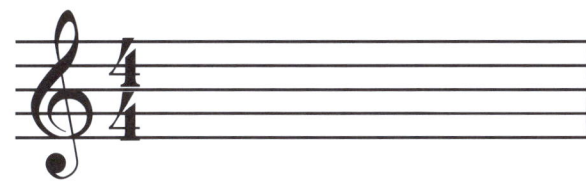

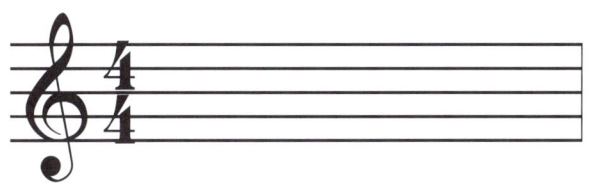

Level 2

QUIZ

(This exercise is to be assisted by the teacher.)

Look at the tune below and answer the questions orally.

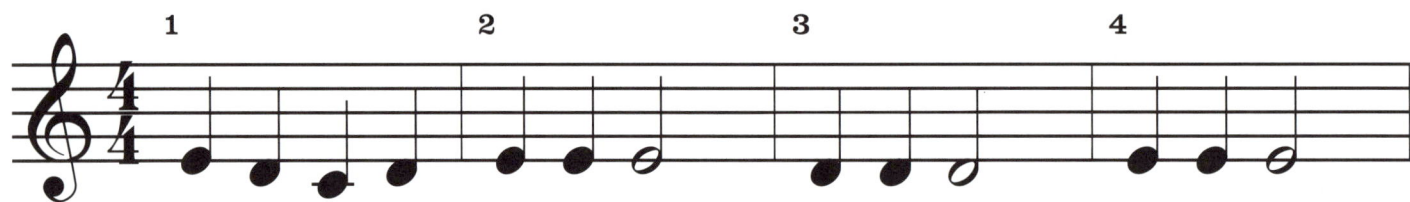

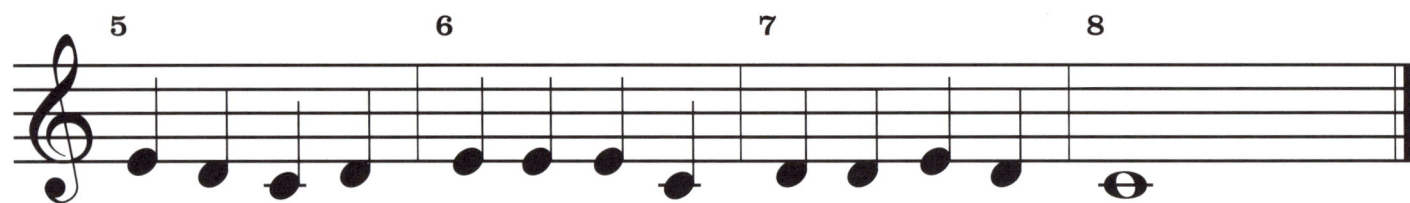

1. Sing the entire tune using note letter-names as lyrics.

2. What is the name of the clef?

3. How many counts are there in each bar?

4. In which bars can you find only crotchet notes?

5. Which bar has only a semibreve note?

6. How many minim notes are there in the whole tune?

7. How many counts is the last note?

8. How many times do you see this rhythm  ?

9. In which bars can you find this melody?

Level 2

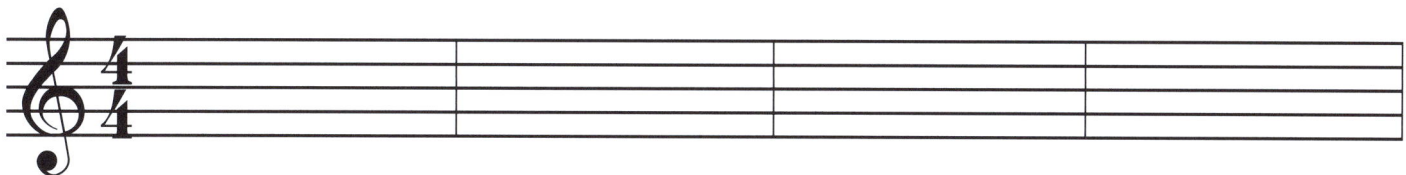

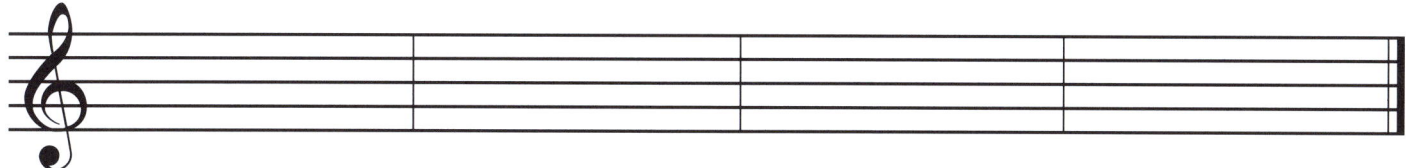

THIS IS TO CERTIFY THAT

....

HAS SUCCESSFULLY COMPLETED

THEORY MADE EASY FOR LITTLE CHILDREN LEVEL 2

AND MAY PROCEED TO

MY FIRST THEORY BOOK

BY LINA NG

A picture of yourself with your musical instrument

NAME : .... TEACHER : ....
                                          (   )
DATE OF BIRTH : ....

AGE : .... DATE : ....